Printing *&* Publishing in the Colonial Era of the United States

Sponsored by

R. R. BOWKER
a division of REED PUBLISHING (USA), INC.

with additional funding from

FINCH, PRUYN & COMPANY, INC. *and*

THE EQUITABLE FOUNDATION

PUBLISHED IN

CONJUNCTION WITH THE EXHIBITION

The Book in the Americas

ORGANIZED BY THE

JOHN CARTER BROWN LIBRARY

AND PRESENTED AT THE

AMERICAS SOCIETY ART GALLERY, NEW YORK

25 JANUARY TO 31 MARCH

1990

Printing & Publishing in the Colonial Era of the United States

A SUPPLEMENT TO *The Book in the Americas* (1988)

WITH A CHECKLIST OF THE ITEMS

IN THAT CATALOGUE

by

NORMAN FIERING AND

SUSAN L. NEWBURY

PROVIDENCE · RHODE ISLAND

THE JOHN CARTER BROWN LIBRARY

MCM · LXXXX

COPYRIGHT © 1990
BY THE JOHN CARTER BROWN LIBRARY

THE JOHN CARTER BROWN LIBRARY IS AN INDEPENDENTLY
FUNDED AND ADMINISTERED CENTER FOR ADVANCED RESEARCH IN
THE HUMANITIES AT BROWN UNIVERSITY

NOT TO BE REPRODUCED IN ANY FORM, IN PART OR WHOLE,
WITHOUT PERMISSION. CORRESPONDENCE SHOULD
BE DIRECTED TO THE JOHN CARTER BROWN
LIBRARY, BOX 1894, PROVIDENCE,
RHODE ISLAND 02912

★

PRINTED IN THE UNITED STATES OF AMERICA
BY MERIDEN-STINEHOUR PRESS, LUNENBURG, VERMONT

CONTENTS

LIST OF ILLUSTRATIONS	*page* ix
PREFACE, *by George W. Landau*	xi
INTRODUCTION, *by Norman Fiering*	xiii
Printing *&* Publishing in the Colonial Era of the United States	1
MASSACHUSETTS	3
PENNSYLVANIA	8
NEW YORK	12
VIRGINIA	15
SELECTED SOURCES	19
BIBLIOGRAPHICAL APPENDIX, *by Susan L. Newbury*	21
PREFACE	23
REFERENCES	25
KEY TO LOCATION SYMBOLS	27
BIBLIOGRAPHICAL DESCRIPTIONS	29
CHECKLIST *of the Seventy-three Items in the Original "Book in the Americas" Exhibition*	33

ILLUSTRATIONS

1. Bay Psalm Book (Cambridge, Mass., 1640).   *pages* 4–5
2. Eliot Indian Bible (Cambridge, Mass., 1663).   6
3. New England Map from William Hubbard, *A narrative of the troubles* (Boston, 1677).   7
4. *Laws of the Province of Pennsilvania* (Philadelphia, 1714).   8
5. German Bible (Germantown, 1743).   9
6. *M. T. Cicero's Cato major* (Philadelphia, 1744).   10
7. *A Manual of Catholic prayers* (Philadelphia, 1774).   11
8. *Charter of the city of New-York* (New York, 1735).   12
9. *Prayers for Shabbath, Rosh-Hashanah* (New York, 5526 [i.e., 1765–1766]).   13
10. Markland, *Typographia* (Williamsburg, 1730).   14
11. College of William and Mary. *The charter, and statutes* (Williamsburg, 1736).   15
12. Thomas Jefferson. *A summary view* (Williamsburg, 1774).   17

PREFACE

THIS YEAR marks the 450th anniversary of the beginning of printing in the New World, in Mexico (1539), and the 350th anniversary of the beginning of printing in British America, in Cambridge, Massachusetts (1639). On the occasion of these two anniversaries, the Americas Society is honored to present *The Book in the Americas*, an exhibition organized by the John Carter Brown Library at Brown University, in Providence, Rhode Island.

The importance of this exhibition as a means of illustrating the cultural history of the Americas—especially Latin America—is especially relevant today, as we near the celebration of Columbus's first voyage to the New World. While our contemporary culture increasingly relies on electronic forms of communication, it is of particular interest to look back and examine the impact of literacy and the distribution of books on new and developing societies. As this exhibition and its accompanying publications so amply demonstrate, an examination of the history of printing also provides new perspectives for understanding the complex interrelations between publishing and many other aspects of a culture, including its economics, politics, education, and moral and spiritual values.

It is fitting, and in the continuing tradition of the Americas Society, that we should collaborate with one of our country's finest libraries in order to provide the American public with an exhibition which will foster a deeper understanding and appreciation of significant cultural milestones in our hemisphere.

On behalf of the Americas Society, I offer my sincere thanks to Dr. Norman Fiering, Director and Librarian of the John Carter Brown Library, for his invaluable role in laying the foundations for this project, and to Susan Danforth, Assistant Librarian of the same institution, who coordinated this exhibition. Julie Greer Johnson, Professor at the University of Georgia, must be singled out for her work in developing this project in its early stages, and for her authorship of the exhibition's official catalogue.

This exhibition could not have been made possible without generous funding from R. R. Bowker. We also gratefully acknowledge the support of the Equitable Foundation and Finch, Pruyn & Co. Inc.

Special thanks are due to Fatima Bercht, Director of Visual Arts at the Americas Society, for her vital work in bringing this project to the Americas Society, and for coordinating the exhibition at the Art Gallery. Thanks also to the staff of the Americas Society Visual Arts Department: Louis Grachos, the Associate Director, and Barbara Berger, Assistant to the Director. Finally, we are most indebted to the members of the Visual Arts Advisory Board for their unflagging support and guidance.

GEORGE W. LANDAU
President, Americas Society

INTRODUCTION

THIS PUBLICATION reflects the ongoing development of the John Carter Brown Library's "Book in the Americas" project, which began in June 1987 with an international scholarly conference on the role of books and printing in the development of culture and society in colonial Latin America. The conference was followed a year later by an exhibition and the publication of an accompanying catalogue on the same theme, entitled *The Book in the Americas* (Providence, 1988), written by Professor Julie Greer Johnson of the University of Georgia. Both the conference and the catalogue have generated unusual interest, in part because the current lively scholarship on *livre et société* had until recently been somewhat neglectful of colonial Latin America as compared to some other parts of the world.

From the beginning, the title of the exhibition has been something of a misnomer, for although at the original conference two of the twenty-two papers presented did concern printing in British North America, the exhibition itself and the 1988 catalogue addressed printing and publishing only in colonial Spanish and Portuguese America, thereby leaving out the rest of the early Americas: British, French, and Dutch. There was in fact no printing in any French or Dutch colonies in the New World before the eighteenth century, but in British North America, beginning before the middle of the seventeenth century, there was a considerable output. This *Supplement*, therefore, which documents the expansion of the original exhibition with the inclusion of twelve books printed in British North America, allows us at last to use the term "Americas," as descriptive of the project, with more justification than was possible before.

The original Latin American *Book in the Americas* catalogue was produced to commemorate the 450th anniversary of the beginning of printing in the Western Hemisphere in Mexico in 1539. Similarly, the publication of this *Supplement* on colonial British America is pointed toward the 350th anniversary of the beginning of printing within the area of the present-day United States in Cambridge, Massachusetts, in 1639. It may come as a surprise to "yanquis" that printing and publishing were well established in Spanish America a full century before the first book was printed in an English colony in the New World. Once a press was established in English America, however, growth was rapid. In the first fifty years of operation in Mexico (1539 to 1589), the presses there turned out 106 titles according to the count of José Toribio Medina, whereas between 1639 and 1689, the presses of the British colonies of North America had produced approximately 600 titles, although many of these were quite insubstantial.

It is remarkable that very little effort has been made by historians to study the history of the book in the Americas comparatively. Such studies could compare development over specified periods of time (the first fifty years of printing in each case, for example) or the state of printing and publishing contemporaneously (in the mid-eighteenth-century, for example). This brief introduction is not the proper vehicle for a detailed and thorough comparison, but a few obvious points may quickly be mentioned. Much of the early printing in Mexico and in Massachusetts a century later was religious in nature, and in both settlements a major incentive to publish was the evangelical drive, in particular the desire to convert the Amerindians to Christianity. At the same time, there was also a great deal of sustenance provided for the Euramerican flocks in the form of sermons, theological statements, catechisms, and the like. Two of the greatest accomplishments of printers in the British colonies had no parallel in Catholic Latin America, the production of Bibles, namely, the famous Eliot Indian Language Bible printed in Massachusetts and the Sauer German Bible printed in Pennsylvania. Catholic New Spain favored formulations of Scriptural and Church teachings, *doctrinas*, rather than the Biblical text itself, but many of these religious works produced under Spanish rule were, like the Eliot Bible, in Indian languages.

At analogous periods in the development of both New Spain and New England there were efforts to print and promulgate local and imperial laws, and one finds many close parallels also in the publication of works related to the establishment of universities, the history of wars with the indigenous peoples, the natural history of the New World, and science and literature. With regard to the last, it is curious that in Mexico, Sister Juana Inés de la Cruz (1648–1695), the much praised nun poet and scholar, was referred to by contemporaries as the "Tenth Muse" (see items 23 and 24 in Johnson, *Book in the Americas*), and only shortly before in Massachusetts Anne Dudley Bradstreet (1612?–1672) published a collection of her poetry with the proud title *The Tenth Muse lately sprung up in America* (London, 1650). In content, too, there are many comparisons between Sor Juana and Bradstreet, since both were acutely conscious of their difficult position as women artists in their times and in a rough frontier milieu. It is notable that Bradstreet's *Tenth Muse* was later republished in Boston in 1678 under a different title.

In science, which by its very nature must be universal, there are similar coincidences. The debate over the nature and meaning of comets, fought out in Mexico between Father Eusebio Francisco Kino (1644–1711), who interpreted the comet of 1680–81 as a divine sign, and Don Carlos de Sigüenza y Góngora (1645–1700), who believed comets were "natural" phenomena (see items 22 and 23 in Johnson, *Book in the Americas*), had a perfect counterpart in New England, where Halley's comet of 1682 provoked a spate of publications, including Increase Mather's *Kometographia, or A discourse concerning comets* (Boston, 1683), which recognized that comets are natural objects but also maintained that they might portend calamitous historical events.

The purpose of the "Book in the Americas" project from the start was not merely to celebrate or study the history of New World printing as such; it was rather to study the history of the consequences of the introduction of "the book" into the New World, including all the ramifications and interconnections that the writing, printing, publishing, distribution, exchange, and reading of books implies. As is by now well understood, the study of the book in history must inevitably encompass such topics as the history of literacy and reading, the study of the variety of technologies related to printing, the economics of the publishing trade, and the relationship between elite and popular culture.

For both the Spanish and the English settlements, for example, it is important to remember that many of the most important publications related to, or coming from, the New World were produced in the metropolitan centers of England or Spain. To study colonial printing only would exclude a large part—the major part—of book culture. Roger Williams's *A key into the language of America* (1643), for example, a vocabulary and phrase book of the Narraganset language was published in London, just as Antonio Ruiz de Montoya's *Arte, y bocabulario de la lengua guarani* (1640) (see item 50 in Johnson, *Book in the Americas*) was published in Madrid. Yet it is highly indicative of the complexity of the history of books in the colonial Americas that Montoya's *Arte, y bocabulario* was republished more than eighty years later in 1722–24 at Santa María la Mayor, Paraguay, by the Guarani Indians in one of the famous Jesuit mission communities there (see items 51 and 52 in Johnson, *Book in the Americas*). The point is simply that few generalizations can be made about the state of culture in either the Spanish or the English colonies based solely on the actual printing done locally. Such work was undertaken on the scene rather than executed in the mother country, or transferred to the mother country rather than done locally, for all sorts of special reasons. Certainly for publication in Indian languages there was a definite advantage to publishing locally, where the expertise was.

One final general point related to the matter of American printing should be noted. Although the licensing of printers was everywhere the rule, there was more control over publishing output in the Spanish and Portuguese empires than in the British, and the penalties for antagonizing secular or ecclesiastical authorities by what one put into type were generally harsher in Latin America.

The John Carter Brown Library and the Americas Society are among only a very small number of institutions or organizations whose sole focus is the Western Hemisphere as a whole. In their respective missions, therefore, they are highly complementary. The Americas Society, however, is primarily concerned with contemporary Latin American and Canadian political and economic issues, and with cultural and artistic achievements from Pre-Columbian times to the present, whereas the exclusive concern of the John Carter Brown Library is the history of the hemisphere during the 300-plus years when it was under European colonial rule, from the time of Columbus's voyage to ca. 1825. The Library actively promotes research and publication in this field and has the greatest comprehensive collection in the world of contemporary printed sources relating to the history of the entire area from Hudson Bay to Patagonia. The Americas Society was enthusiastic about the possibility of hosting, in its art gallery, an exhibition of books, thus giving continuity to an ongoing series of exhibitions that examine colonial culture and art.

At an early stage in the organization of the exhibition, we were fortunate to catch the attention of Mr. Stanley Walker, a vice-president at the R. R. Bowker Company. Bowker, the distinguished publisher for the publishing trade since 1872, was planning to celebrate another occasion in 1990, the fiftieth anniversary of the annual publication of *Literary Market Place*, the vademecum of all who work in the publishing industry. On the occasion of this anniversary, Bowker had decided to establish the first national *LMP* Awards to honor excellence and innovation in the field of publishing, to be given annually in eighteen special categories. How appropriate it would be, Mr. Walker thought, to present these awards against the backdrop of an exhibition at the Americas Society that commemorates the very beginnings of publishing in the Western Hemisphere almost a half-millennium ago. Thus Bowker became the sponsor of the exhibition.

This exhibition has been made possible, then, through the close collaboration of the John Carter Brown Library, the Americas Society, and R. R. Bowker. It is a pleasure to acknowledge here the good will and hard work of staff members at every level of all three organizations who have contributed to the success of the enterprise. It is also my pleasure to express the gratitude of the Society and the Library to the donors who have helped to underwrite the exhibition and associated publications: R. R. Bowker, the Equitable Foundation, and Finch, Pruyn & Company, Inc., which as it happens is celebrating in 1990 its own 125th anniversary.

NORMAN FIERING
Director & Librarian
The John Carter Brown Library

Printing & Publishing in the Colonial Era of the United States

PRINTING AND PUBLISHING IN THE COLONIAL ERA OF THE UNITED STATES

MASSACHUSETTS

1.

BAY PSALM BOOK. *The whole booke of Psalmes.* [Cambridge, Mass.], 1640.

The "Bay Psalm Book," the first substantial production of the first press in the English colonies, is one of the most famous of all "rare" books. Eleven copies (not all of which are perfect) have survived of the 1,700 initially printed. There are many books more rare, of which perhaps only one or two copies are known to be extant, but none with greater symbolical weight. Although the literary qualities of this translation into English of the Hebrew psalms from the Old Testament have been faulted, the book must have been a considerable success, for another edition of 2,000 copies was issued by the press at Cambridge in 1651, the work was reprinted in England, and many other editions followed. This copy bears the signature of one of the translators, Richard Mather. Psalmodies were also published in Mexico, some for the use of Indians (see Johnson, *Book in the Americas*, item 13).

2.

BIBLE. Massachuset. Eliot. 1663. *Mamusse wunneetupanatamwe up-Biblum God.* Cambridge, Mass., 1663.

There are few better examples of Puritan energy and determination than the "Eliot Indian Bible," which required oral translation of the entire Bible into the Algonquian tongue of Massachuset, transcription into phonetic English, and then the enormous task of typesetting and printing the whole. Hugh Amory of the Harvard Library has recently speculated that "the 938 reams of paper (over 300,000 sheets) consumed in two editions [1661–1663, 1680–1685] of the [Eliot] Bible probably outweigh all the previous

Richard Mather

10.4.9

quid novi apud te
nichil novi apud me
Quid novi nihil novi
quid novi quid novi
Richardus Matherus
eius liber

Oct. 10, 1848. Examined this
book by the catch word
of every leaf and believe
it to be complete. S.T.A

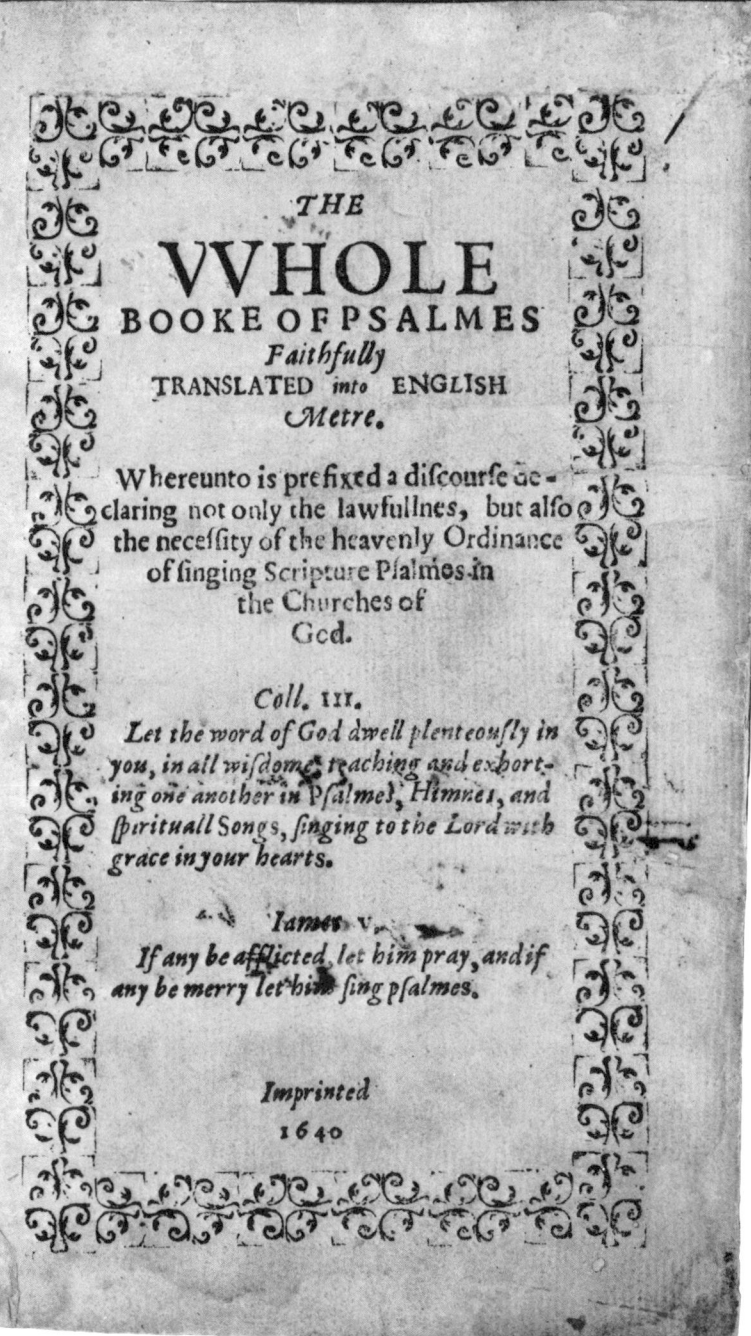

FIG. 1. The signature of Richard Mather, one of the translators of the psalms in this famous book, is visible in the upper part of the left-hand page.

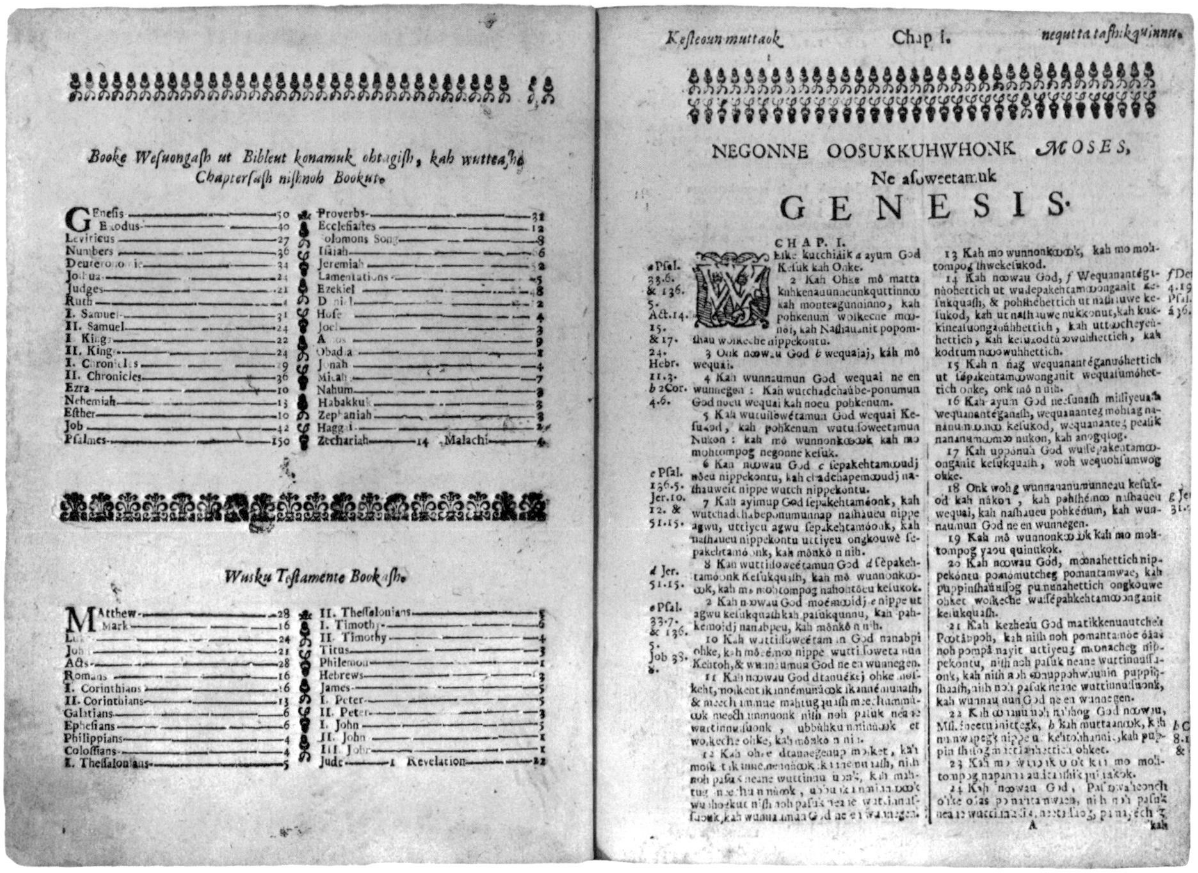

FIG. 2. The Bible translated into an Amerindian language, the first such effort to translate the Bible as a means of evangelization.

printing in [the English colonies] together." John Eliot (1604–1690), a Puritan minister known as the "Apostle to the Indians," was assisted in this huge evangelical task, it is not often mentioned, by Indians provided with a European education. The same phenomenon of collaboration between missionaries and Indians to produce religious works in native languages is found throughout Latin America. See, for example, Maturino Gilberti (1498–1585), *Dialogo de doctrina christiana enla lengua de Mechuacan* (Mexico, 1559), item 11 in Johnson, *Book in the Americas*.

3.

WILLIAM HUBBARD (1621 or 2–1704). *A narrative of the troubles with the Indians in New-England*. Boston, 1677.

There was no shortage of effective wood engraving in Mexico during the nearly 150 years when printing was flourishing there before this history by William Hubbard appeared (see, for example, Francisco Hernández [1514–1587], *Quatros libros* [Mexico,

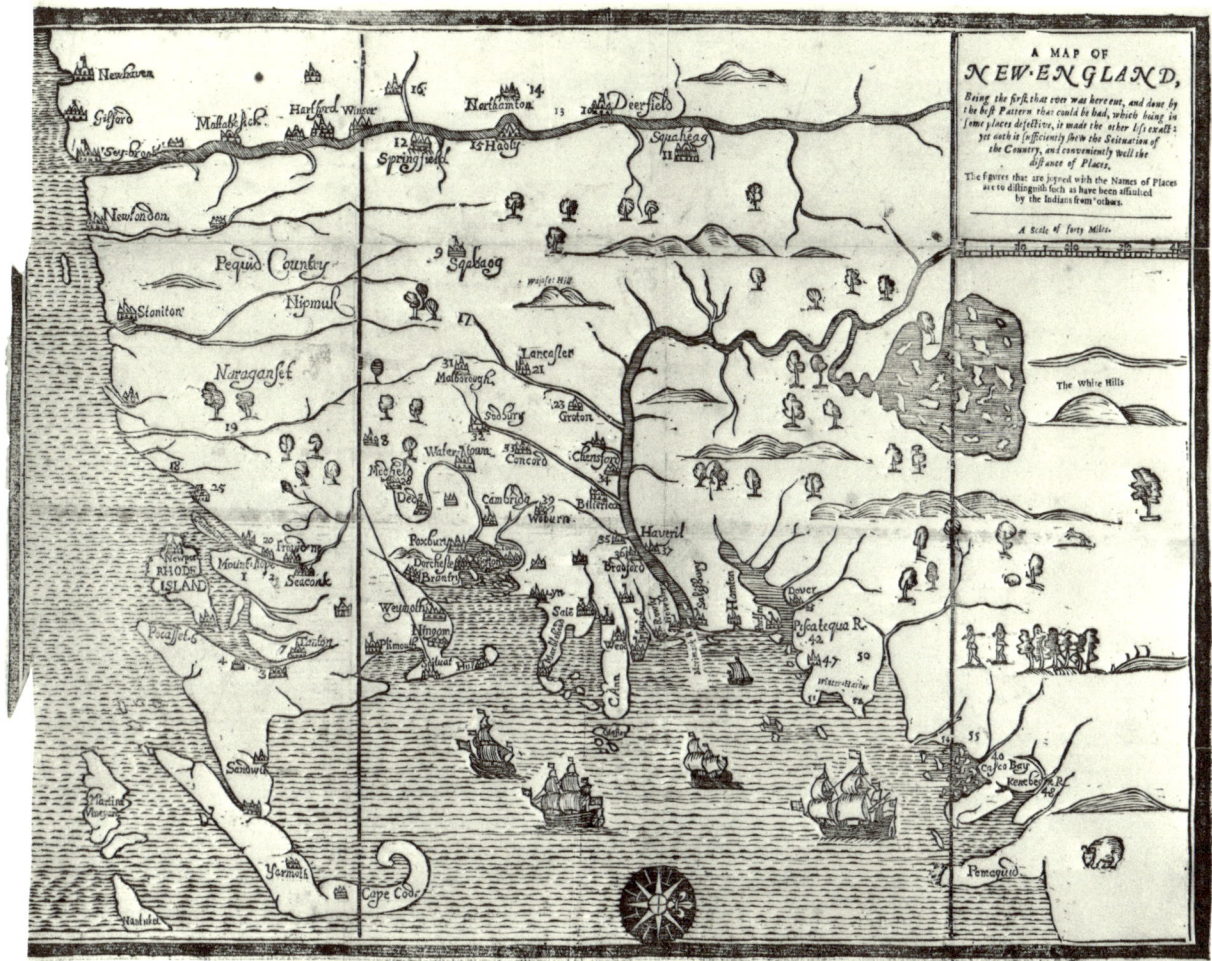

FIG. 3. This map from William Hubbard's *Narrative of the Troubles with the Indians* (Boston, 1677) was the first printed in British North America.

1615], item 17 in Johnson, *Book in the Americas*). However, the map of New England shown here, produced by John Foster of Boston, may have been the first map to be cut and published in the Western Hemisphere. It was certainly the first map engraved and published in the British colonies. The Spanish government in the sixteenth and seventeenth centuries was notoriously guarded about revealing geographical information concerning its American territories that might prove useful to enemies. This caution perhaps accounts for the absence of maps in early Mexican imprints.

FIG. 4. The first printing of the laws of Pennsylvania, beginning with the year 1700.

4.

PENNSYLVANIA (Colony). *The laws of the Province of Pennsylvania collected into one volumn [sic].* Philadelphia, 1714.

One of the common functions of colonial presses everywhere, aside from the printing of religious works, was the secular task of supporting government through the printing of laws. *Ordenanças y copilacion de leyes* (Mexico, 1548) was the first law book printed in the New World, less than ten years after the press in Mexico was founded and its sixteenth issue (see item 5 in Johnson, *Book in the Americas*). In Massachusetts, also, the first printing of the *Book of general lawes and libertyes* (Cambridge, Mass., 1648) occurred less than a decade after the start-up of printing in the province and was the tenth surviving issue of the press. The work displayed here is the first publication of the collected laws of Pennsylvania, which appeared twenty-nine years after the origins of printing in the colony. It was printed by Andrew Bradford, the son of the first printer in Pennsylvania, William Bradford, who began printing there in 1685.

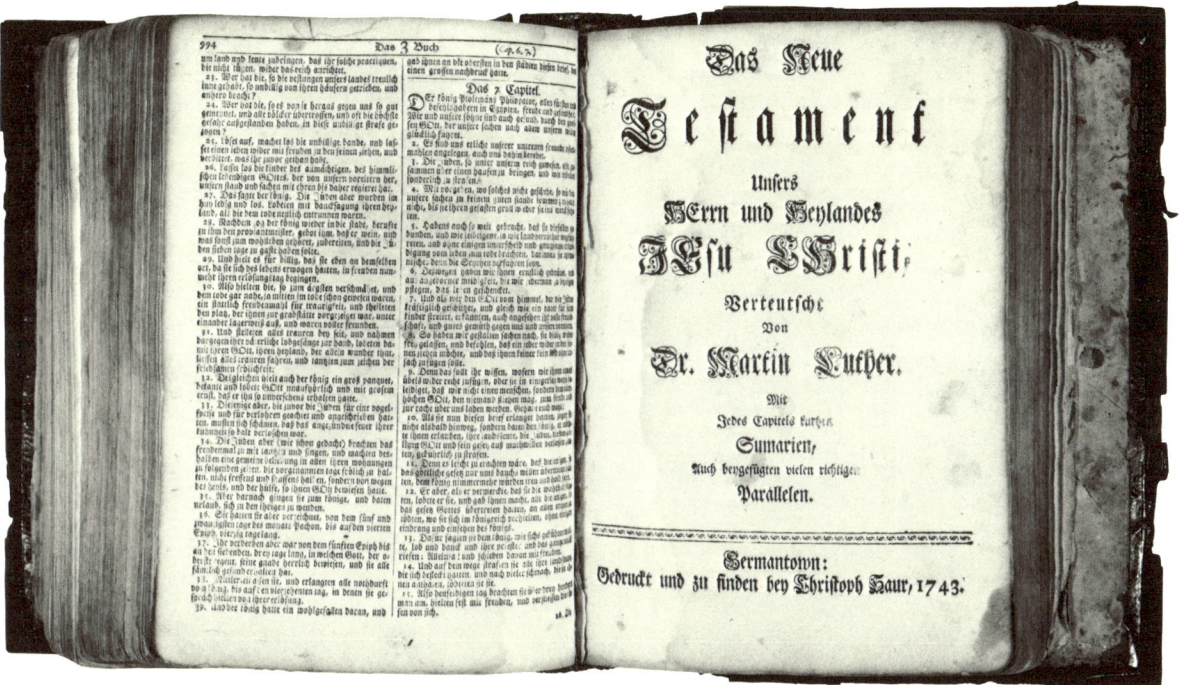

FIG. 5. The famous Sauer Bible, the first Bible printed in the Western Hemisphere in a European language.

5.

BIBLE. German. Luther. 1743. *Biblia, das ist: Die Heilige Schrift Altes und Neues Testaments*. Germantown, 1743.

The first Bible printed in the Western Hemisphere was Eliot's Indian Bible (see number 2 above). The first Bible printed in the Western Hemisphere in a European language was Christopher Sauer's German Bible, published in 1743 and hardly less gargantuan a feat of typesetting and printing than Eliot's Bible. German-language printing in the colonial United States was in general a big enterprise, with no less than 509 titles having been issued in German between 1728 and 1778. In fact, the largest book published in the British colonies before the Revolution, indeed in the Western Hemisphere, was *Der blutige Schau-Platz*, the Mennonite book of martyrs printed by the Ephrata brotherhood in 1748–1749, a copy of which is also in the John Carter Brown Library. It is 1,512 pages long. The remarkable multiplicity and diversity of publishing in the United States was foreshadowed by these beginnings in Pennsylvania.

M. T. CICERO's
CATO MAJOR,
OR HIS
DISCOURSE
OF
OLD-AGE:
With Explanatory NOTES.

PHILADELPHIA:
Printed and Sold by B. FRANKLIN,
MDCCXLIV.

FIG. 6. The title-page of this translation of Cicero by the learned Philadelphian James Logan is in two colors.

6.

MARCUS TULLIUS CICERO. *M. T. Cicero's Cato major, or his Discourse of old-age.* Philadelphia, 1744.

This work, a translation into English of Cicero's *De senectute* by the distinguished Philadelphia polymath James Logan (1674–1751), is often cited as the most elegant product typographically of Benjamin Franklin's press. Among other things, this book represents the devotion to the ancient Classics that was pervasive in the colonial Americas. Neither Spanish Catholic nor English Protestant piety, both of which at times wished to suppress the avid study of the Greek and Roman pagans, made much headway against the enthusiasm for the Classics. The earliest translation of a Classical author's work to be published in the New World was Alphonsus, a Vera Cruce's translation into Latin of Aristotle's *Categoriae*, issued as *Dialectica resolutio* (Mexico, 1554) (see item 6 in Johnson, *Book in the Americas*).

7.

A Manual of Catholic prayers. Philadelphia, 1774.

When one considers the Western Hemisphere as a whole, Roman Catholicism was by far the dominant religion brought to the New World in the early period. Even in British

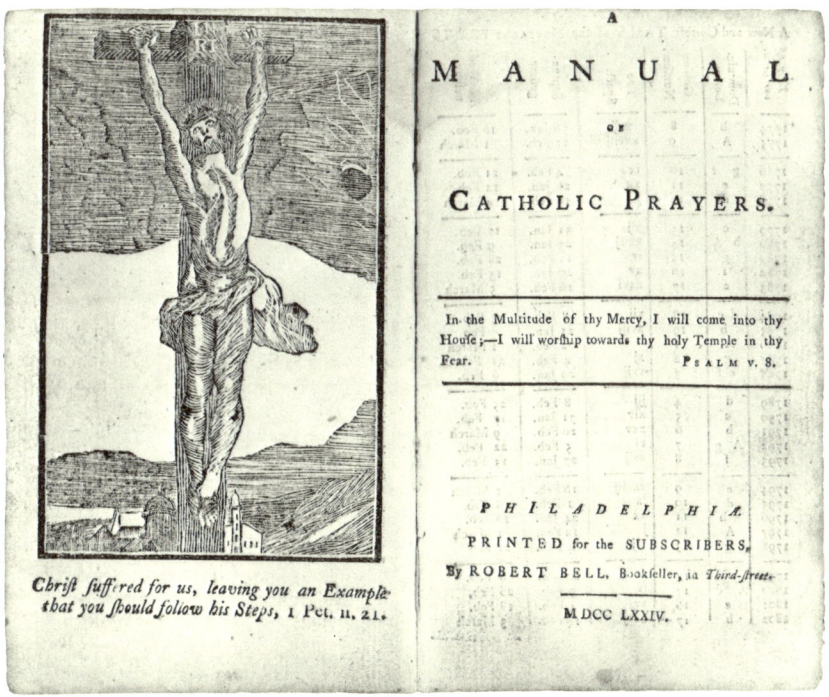

FIG. 7. This work is one of the earliest printed evidences of the Roman Catholic presence in British North America.

North America, where hostility to "papists" was a powerful force, there were settlements of Catholics, first in Maryland and later in Rhode Island and Pennsylvania. The work shown, one of the earliest Roman Catholic publications in the colonial United States, was the accommodating response of a printer to the realities of religious diversity in Pennsylvania. Insofar as the work is Roman Catholic, it is a link to Spanish America; insofar as it represents religious diversity, it is in sharp contrast to the development of Spanish civilization in Latin America.

NEW YORK

8.

NEW YORK (N.Y.). *The charter of the city of New-York.* New York, 1735.

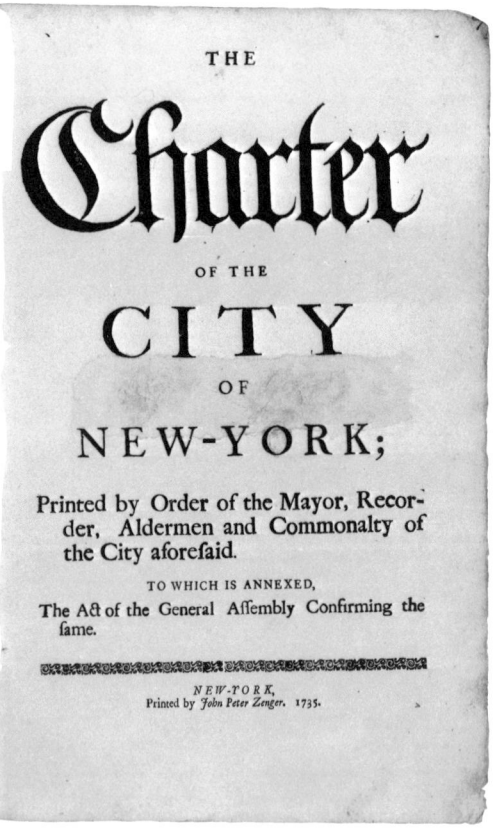

No review of the history of printing and publishing in New York can omit some reference to John Peter Zenger (1697–1746), the German-born printer who has become a symbol of freedom of the press. Zenger came to America in 1710 and after gaining experience as an apprentice and journeyman, opened his own printing business in 1726. He became the editor and publisher of the *New-York Weekly Journal*, which took a position critical of the administration of Governor William Cosby. In 1734 Cosby had Zenger arrested, held incommunicado for almost a year, and brought to trial in 1735 for seditious libel. Zenger's lawyer, Andrew Hamilton of Philadelphia, successfully pleaded that truth was a defense in libel cases, an argument of fundamental importance in the development of freedom to publish in the United States. The *Charter of the city of New-York*, printed by Zenger immediately after his acquittal, is regarded as one of his most craftsmanlike publications.

FIG. 8. Much of the early printing in the Americas related to local affairs, such as this printing by Peter Zenger of the New York City charter.

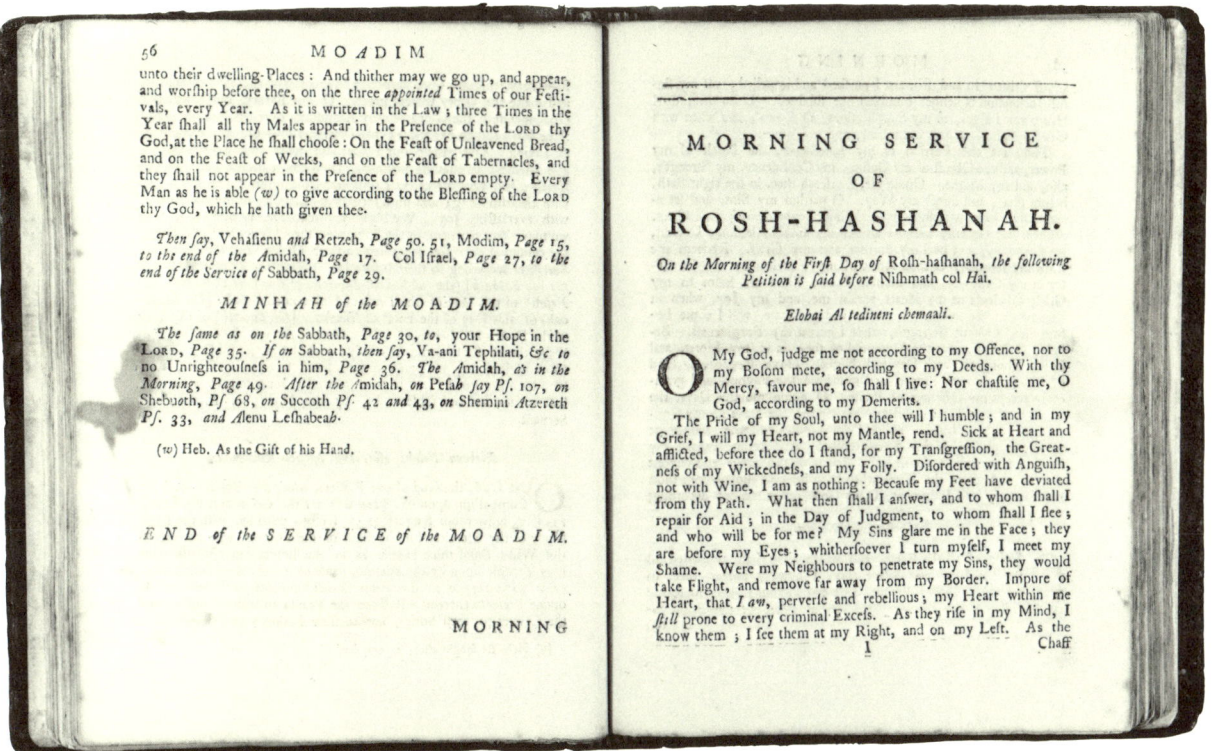

FIG. 9. Judaism in British North America was so well-established by the time this prayer book was published in New York in 1765–1766, that translation into English from Hebrew seemed needed.

9.

SABBATH PRAYERS (Sephardic). English. *Prayers for Shabbath, Rosh-Hashanah, and Kippur, or The Sabbath, the begining [sic] of the year, and the Day of Atonements . . . According to the order of the Spanish and Portuguese Jews.* Translated by Isaac Pinto. New York, 5526. [i.e., 1765–1766]

One of the few direct links between Spanish and Portuguese America and English America in the early colonial period, other than warfare in the Caribbean, was the migration of the Sephardic Jews, who first came to Dutch-controlled New York in 1654 from Curaçao. A series of Inquisitions in Mexico, Peru, and Brazil throughout the seventeenth and eighteenth centuries destroyed whatever Jewish culture was covertly transported to Latin America, but in the English colonies, particularly in New York and Rhode Island, publications by the Jewish community were able to appear. The work shown here, prepared by Isaac Pinto, a merchant whose native language was Portuguese, was the first Jewish prayer book printed in the Americas. Pinto made this translation because, he said, Hebrew is "imperfectly understood by many, by some, not at all," and it is "necessary to translate our Prayers into the Language of the Country wherein it has pleased divine Providence to appoint our Lot."

TYPOGRAPHIA.
AN
ODE,
ON
PRINTING.

I.

YE NYMPHS, who o'er *Castalian* Springs,
    With joint Command preside,
Who trill the Lyre's sonorous Strings,
Record the great and glorious Things,
Of Godlike *Rulers*, matchless *Kings*,
    And poetic Numbers guide;
    Daughters of eternal *Jove*,
    Gently to my Assistance move:

B   Whether

FIG. 10. It must have been an enjoyable task for the printer of this work, William Parks, working in Williamsburg, Virginia, in 1730, to typeset and print this ode to his craft.

10.

JOHN MARKLAND. *Typographia. An ode, on printing*. Williamsburg, 1730.

The second book to come from William Parks's Williamsburg press was this paean to the art of printing itself. It is, in fact, the first work of any kind on the subject of printing to be published in English America (perhaps in the entire hemisphere) and also the first poem published in Virginia. This is the only copy of *Typographia* known to have survived. The very earliest book of poetry written by an American author and published in America was *Arauco domado* by Pedro de Oña (1570?–1643?), printed in Lima by Antonio Ricardo in 1596. Oña was one of Chile's first poets. (See item 40 in Johnson, *Book in the Americas*.) The first book of poetry published in British America could be said to be the Bay Psalm Book, followed by Michael Wigglesworth's *Day of Doom* (Cambridge, Mass., 1662).

11.

COLLEGE OF WILLIAM AND MARY. *The charter, and statutes, of the College of William and Mary, in Virginia*. Williamsburg, 1736.

Some of the earliest printing throughout the New World relates to colonial colleges. The first publication of the laws of Harvard College appeared in a work entitled *New*

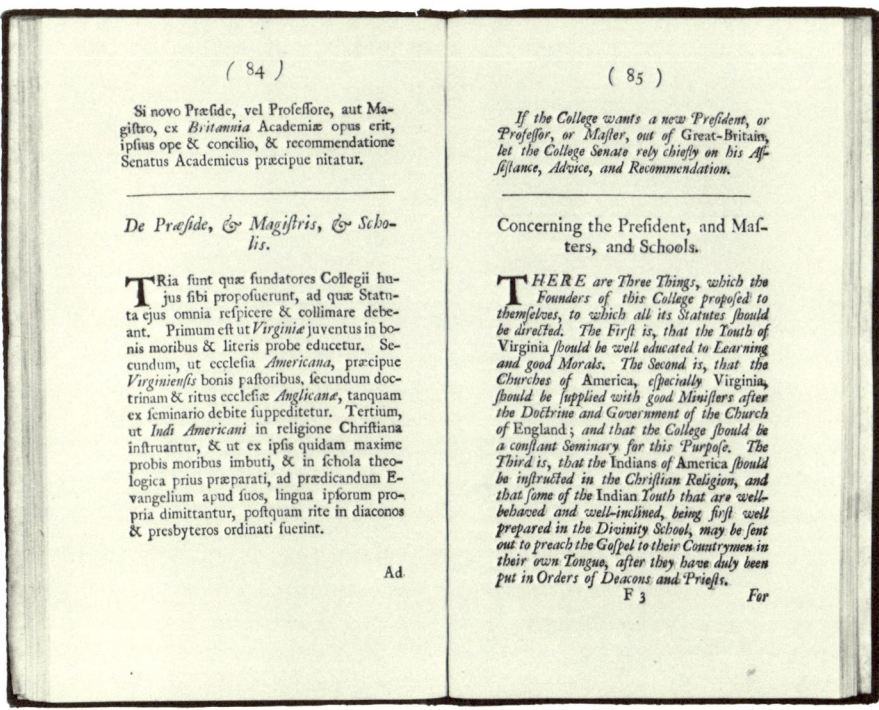

FIG. 11. The educational goals of the College of William and Mary are well-stated in these pages from *The charter, and statutes, of the College . . .* (Williamsburg, 1736).

Englands first fruits, published in London in 1643, followed by the *Laws and orders of Harvard College* (Cambridge, Mass., 1655). The first universities in Latin America date back to the 1550s, and the *Constituciones y ordenanças* of the University of San Marcos were published in Lima in 1602 (see item 38 in Johnson, *Book in the Americas*). Like the *Typographia*, above, this printing of the laws of William and Mary is extremely rare, with only four extant copies recorded in the bibliographical literature.

12.

THOMAS JEFFERSON (1743–1826). *A summary view of the rights of British America.* Williamsburg, [1774].

There are many parallels between the movement for independence in colonial British America in the 1770s and those in Latin America in the 1820s. The John Carter Brown Library has both the most complete collection in the world of contemporary political pamphlets relating to the growth and aftermath of the United States revolution and a major collection of materials relating to the revolutions in Latin America. The Enlightenment political ideology that inspired Thomas Jefferson is analogous to that which inspired the South American liberators (see, for example, items 46 and 47 in Johnson, *Book in the Americas*), and as is well known, the revolution of the thirteen U.S. colonies served as an example to the revolutionary leaders in Latin America. This classic political statement by Thomas Jefferson, drafted as instructions for the guidance of the Virginia delegation to the Continental Congress, was published by friends of Jefferson without his knowledge. The work was reprinted in Philadelphia and in London.

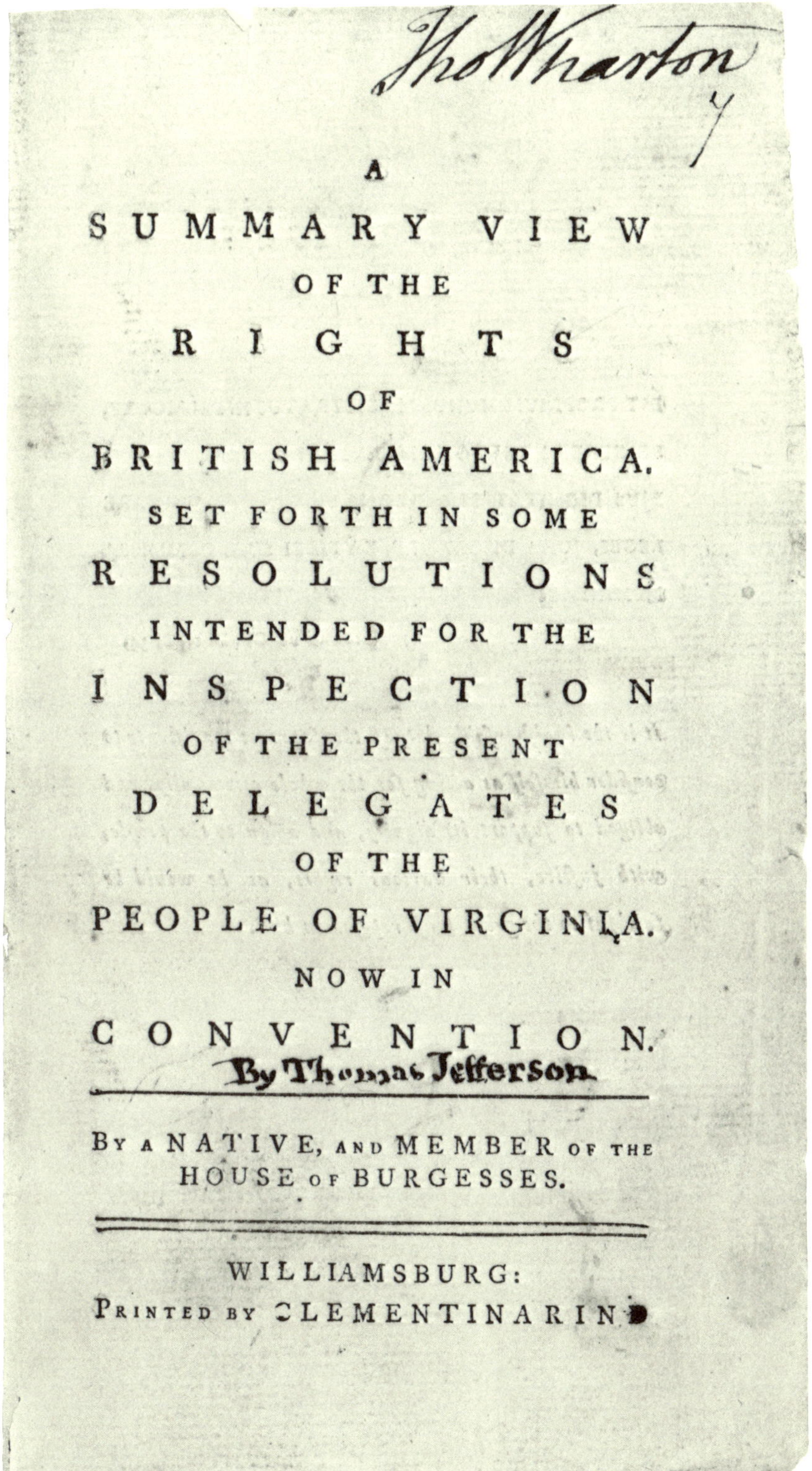

Tho Wharton

A
SUMMARY VIEW
OF THE
RIGHTS
OF
BRITISH AMERICA,
SET FORTH IN SOME
RESOLUTIONS
INTENDED FOR THE
INSPECTION
OF THE PRESENT
DELEGATES
OF THE
PEOPLE OF VIRGINIA.
NOW IN
CONVENTION.
By Thomas Jefferson

BY A NATIVE, AND MEMBER OF THE
HOUSE OF BURGESSES.

WILLIAMSBURG:
PRINTED BY CLEMENTINA RIND

FIG. 12. This important statement by Thomas Jefferson of the rights of colonists in British North America was published by friends and admirers of Jefferson without the author's knowledge.

SELECTED SOURCES

for the Study of Printing & Publishing in the Colonial Era of the United States

There is a vast literature on this subject, and it is constantly being added to. The list below includes only a few general works that will lead the reader to more specialized research and a few specific references that were used in preparation of the text of this catalogue. The standard bibliographies are listed on pp. 25–26, below. We wish to thank Mr. William Reese for his valuable comments on an early draft of this catalogue.

AMORY, Hugh. *First Impressions: Printing in Cambridge, 1639–1989* (Cambridge, Mass.: Harvard University, 1989)

BÖTTE, Gerd-J., and Werner TANNHOF. *The First Century of German Language Printing in the United States of America . . .* (Göttingen: Niedersächsische Staats- und Universitätsbibliothek, 1989).

BOYD, Julian, ed. *The Papers of Thomas Jefferson.* Vol. 1 (Princeton, N.J., 1950)

PESTANA, Carla G. *Liberty of Conscience and the Growth of Religious Diversity in Early America, 1636–1786.* Foreword by Martin E. Marty (Providence: John Carter Brown Library, 1986); and Helena Costa, *Liberty of Conscience: Bibliographical Supplement* (Providence: John Carter Brown Library, 1986)

REESE, William S. *The Printers' First Fruits. An Exhibition of Imprints, 1640–1742, from the Collections of the American Antiquarian Society* (Worcester, Mass.: American Antiquarian Society, 1989).

TANSELLE, G. Thomas. *A Guide to the Study of United States Imprints* (Cambridge: Harvard University Press, 1971).

WROTH, Lawrence C. *The Colonial Printer* (Portland, Maine: The Southworth-Anthoensen Press, 1938 [2nd ed.]).

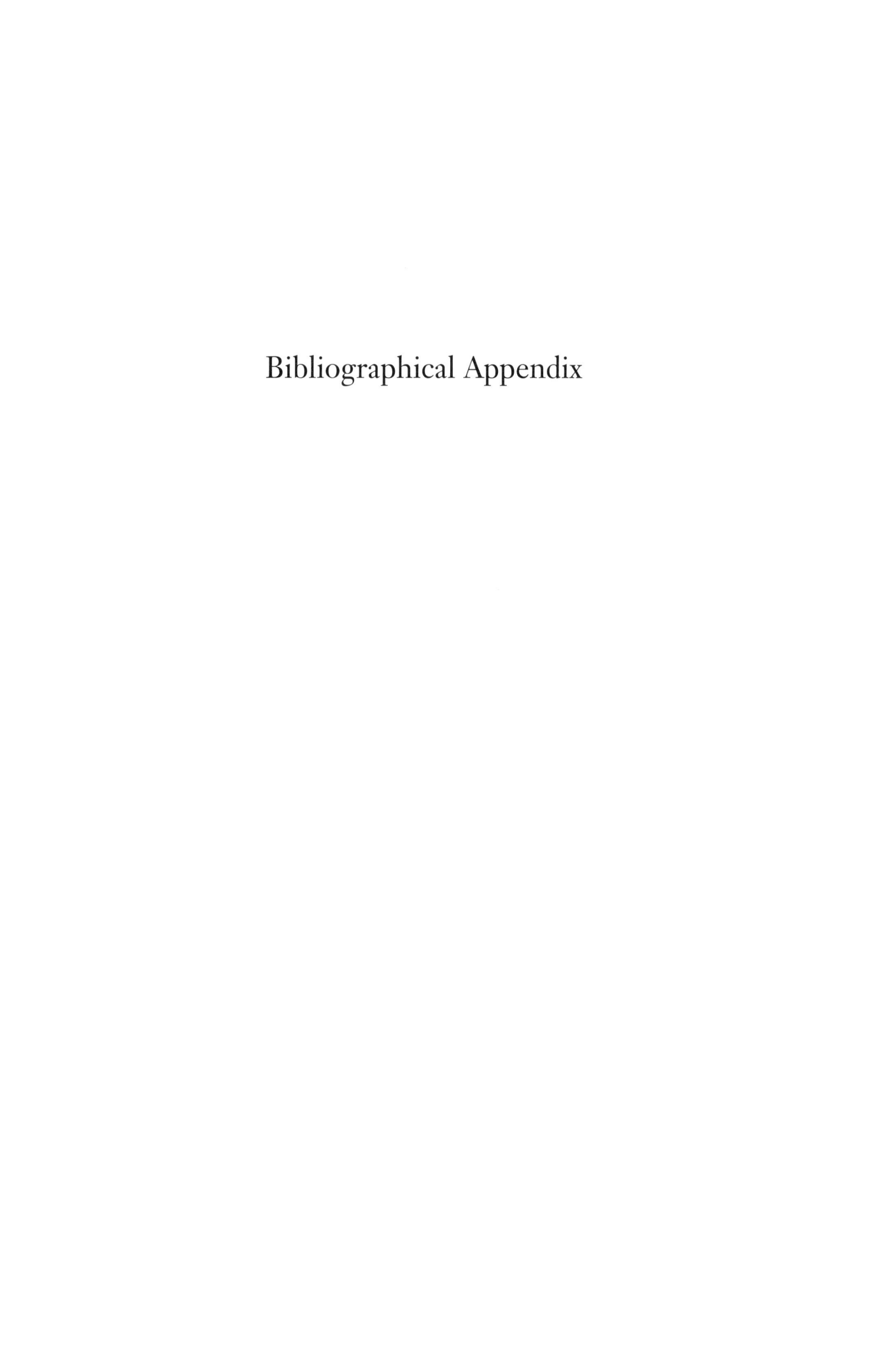

Bibliographical Appendix

PREFACE

THE Bibliographical Appendix is meant to provide a detailed description of the physical characteristics of each of the twelve books in this *Supplement*. The works are arranged alphabetically by main entry: author, title, or corporate body. Reference numbers preceding each item link them to the *Supplement* itself. The descriptions of each work are governed by the *Anglo-American Cataloguing Rules* (2nd edition) and the *Bibliographic Description of Rare Books*, with some modifications in format. All of the bibliographic material presented here will also be entered into the automated information retrieval system known as RLIN (Research Libraries Information Network) and thus will be available to RLIN subscribers nationwide.

In addition, each description contains abbreviated references to published bibliographies, and a list of these sources has been provided for those seeking further information on a particular work. Location symbols for copies in the United States are also included for each book. These symbols represent libraries and institutions which have contributed cards to the *National Union Catalog, Pre-1956 Imprints*. (For item 1, the *Bay Psalm Book*, the census of copies was taken from Hugh Amory, *First Impressions: Printing in Cambridge, 1639–1989*. [Cambridge, Mass., 1989].)

As previously indicated, this *Supplement* augments the exhibition catalogue by Julie Greer Johnson, *The Book in the Americas: the Role of Books and Printing in the Development of Culture and Society in Colonial Latin America* (Providence, 1988). For that reason, an alphabetical checklist of the seventy-three items found in the original catalogue is also included here.

This Bibliographical Appendix has greatly benefitted from the cataloguing expertise of Dr. Günther Buchheim as well as the computer assistance of Mrs. Lynne Harrell, and I wish to express my gratitude to each of them.

SUSAN L. NEWBURY
Chief of Cataloguing
The John Carter Brown Library

REFERENCES

ADAMS, *Amer. pamphlets*
Adams, Thomas Randolph. *American independence, the growth of an idea: a bibliographical study of the American political pamphlets printed between 1764 and 1776 dealing with the dispute between Great Britain and her colonies.* Providence: Brown University Press, 1965.

ADAMS, *Brit. pamphlets*
Adams, Thomas Randolph. *The American controversy: a bibliographical study of the British pamphlets about the American disputes, 1764–1783.* Providence: Brown University Press; New York: Bibliographical Society, 1980.

BERG, *18th cent. Williamsburg imprints*
Berg, Susan Stromei. *Eighteenth-century Williamsburg imprints.* New York: Clearwater Pub. Co., 1986.

BÖTTE & TANNHOF
Bötte, Gerd-J., and Werner Tannhof. *The first century of German language printing in the United States of America: a bibliography based on the studies of Oswald Seidensticker and Wilbur H. Oda.* Göttingen: Niedersächsische Staats- und Universitätsbibliothek, 1989.

BRISTOL
Bristol, Roger Pattrell. *Supplement to Charles Evans' American bibliography.* Charlottesville: Published for the Bibliographical Society of America and the Bibliographical Society of the University of Virginia [by] University Press of Virginia, 1970.

CHURCH, *Discovery*
Church, Elihu Dwight. *A catalogue of books relating to the discovery and early history of North and South America forming a part of the library of E. D. Church.* Comp. and annotated by George Watson Cole. New York: Dodd, Mead & Co.; Cambridge: University Press, 1907.

CLAYTON-TORRENCE, *A trial bib. of colonial Virginia*
Virginia State Library. *A trial bibliography of colonial Virginia. Special report of the Department of Bibliography, William Clayton-Torrence, bibliographer.* Richmond: D. Bottom, Superintendent of Public Printing, 1908–1910.

DARLOW, *Holy Scripture*
British and Foreign Bible Society. *Historical catalogue of the printed editions of Holy Scripture in the library of the British and Foreign Bible Society.* Comp. by T. H. Darlow, M.A. and H. F. Moule. London: The Bible House, 1903–1911.

EVANS
Evans, Charles. *American bibliography: a chronological dictionary of all books, pamphlets and periodical publications printed in the United States of America from the genesis of printing in 1639 down to and including the year 1820.* New York: P. Smith, 1941–1955 (Vol. 13 repr. 1962).

FINOTTI, *Bib. catholica americana*
Finotti, Joseph Maria. *Bibliographia catholica americana: a list of works written by Catholic authors, and published in the United States.* New York: The Catholic Publication House, 1872.

GREEN, *John Foster*
Green, Samuel Abbott. *John Foster, the earliest American engraver and the first Boston printer.* Boston: Massachusetts Historical Society, 1909.

HILDEBURN, *The issues of the press in Pennsylvania*
Hildeburn, Charles Swift Riché. *A century of printing. The issues of the press in Pennsylvania, 1685–1784.* Philadelphia: [Press of Matlack & Harvey], 1885–1886.

HOLMES, *Minor Mathers*
Holmes, Thomas James. *The minor Mathers, a list of their works.* Cambridge, Mass.: Harvard University Press, 1940.

J. C. BROWN, CAT., 1493–1800
Brown, John Carter. *Bibliotheca Americana: a catalogue of books relating to North and South America in the library of John Carter Brown of Providence, R.I.* Providence: Printed by H. O. Houghton & Co., Cambridge, 1865–1871.

J. C. BROWN, CAT., 1482–1700
Brown, John Carter. *Bibliotheca Americana: a catalogue of books relating to North and South America in the library of the late John Carter Brown of Providence, R. I.* Providence: Printed by H. O. Houghton & Co., Cambridge, 1875–1882.

JCB LIB., *Annual reports*
Brown University. John Carter Brown Library. *Annual reports.* Providence: The Library, 1901–1975 (Years 1901–1966, repr., with index, The Library, 1972.)

JCB LIB. CAT., PRE-1675
Brown University. John Carter Brown Library. *Bibliotheca Americana: catalogue of the John Carter Brown*

Library in Brown University, Providence, Rhode Island. 3rd ed. Providence: The Library, 1919–1931.

MILLER, *Benjamin Franklin's Philadelphia printing*
Miller, Clarence William. *Benjamin Franklin's Philadelphia printing, 1728–1766: a descriptive bibliography.* Philadelphia: American Philosophical Society, 1974.

MURPHY, *John Holt*
Murphy, Layton Barnes. *John Holt, patriot printer and publisher.* [Microfilm copy of a thesis: University of Michigan] Ann Arbor: University Microfilms, [1965].

O'CALLAGHAN, *Holy Scriptures*
O'Callaghan, Edmund Bailey. *A list of editions of the Holy Scriptures, and parts thereof, printed in America previous to 1860: with introduction and bibliographical notes.* Albany: Munsell & Rowland, 1861.

PARSONS, *Catholic Americana*
Parsons, Wilfrid. *Early Catholic Americana; a list of books and other works by Catholic authors in the United States, 1729–1830.* New York: Macmillan, 1939.

PILLING, *Bib. Algonquian languages*
Pilling, James Constantine. *Bibliography of the Algonquian languages.* Washington, D.C.: U.S. Government Printing Office, 1891.

RUMBALL-PETRE, *America's first Bibles*
Rumball-Petre, Edwin Alfred Robert. *America's first Bibles, with a census of 555 extant Bibles.* Portland, Me.: The Southworth-Anthoensen Press, 1940.

RUTHERFURD, *John Peter Zenger*
Rutherfurd, Livingston. *John Peter Zenger, his press, his trial and a bibliography of Zenger imprints.* New York: Dodd, Mead & Co., 1904.

SABIN
Sabin, Joseph. *Bibliotheca Americana; a dictionary of books relating to America from its discovery to the present time.* Begun by Joseph Sabin, continued by Wilberforce Eames and completed by R.W.G. Vail, for the Bibliographical Society of America. New York: Sabin, 1868–1892; Bibliographical Society of America, 1928–1936. (Repr., Amsterdam: N. Israel, 1961–1962.)

SEIDENSTICKER, *German printing*
Seidensticker, Oswald. *The first century of German printing in America, 1728–1830; preceded by a notice of the literary work of F. D. Pastorius.* Philadelphia: Schaefer & Koradi, 1893.

STC
Pollard, Alfred William, and Gilbert Richard Redgrave. *A short-title catalogue of books printed in England, Scotland & Ireland and of English books printed abroad, 1475–1640.* London: The Bibliographical Society, 1926.

WING
Wing, Donald Goddard. *Short-title catalogue of books printed in England, Scotland, Ireland, Wales, and British America, and of English books printed in other countries, 1641–1700.* New York: Index Society, 1945–1951.

WRIGHT, *Early Bibles of America*
Wright, John. *Early Bibles of America.* New York: T. Whittaker, 1892.

KEY TO LOCATION SYMBOLS

CALIFORNIA
CSmH   Henry E. Huntington Library, San Marino

CONNECTICUT
CtHT-W   Trinity College, Hartford, Watkinson Library
CtY   Yale University, New Haven

DISTRICT OF COLUMBIA
DGU   Georgetown University Library
DLC   U.S. Library of Congress

ILLINOIS
ICN   Newberry Library, Chicago

INDIANA
InU   Indiana University, Bloomington

MARYLAND
MdBJ-G   Johns Hopkins University, John Work Garrett Library

MASSACHUSETTS
MB   Boston Public Library
MH   Harvard University, Cambridge
MH-L   Harvard University, Law School Library
MHi   Massachusetts Historical Society, Boston
MNF   Forbes Library, Northampton
MWA   American Antiquarian Society, Worcester
MWelC   Wellesley College, Wellesley
MWiW-C   Williams College, Williamstown, Chapin Library

MICHIGAN
MiD   Detroit Public Library
MiU-C   University of Michigan, William L. Clements Library

MINNESOTA
MnU   University of Minnesota, Minneapolis

MISSOURI
MoSCS   Concordia Seminary Library, St. Louis

NEW JERSEY
NjP   Princeton University, Princeton

NEW YORK
N   New York State Library, Albany
NCaS   St. Lawrence University, Canton
NHi   New-York Historical Society, New York
NIC   Cornell University, Ithaca
NN   New York Public Library
NNAB   American Bible Society, New York
NNC   Columbia University, New York

NORTH CAROLINA
NcD   Duke University, Durham
NcWSW   Wake Forest College, Winston-Salem

OHIO
OC   Public Library of Cincinnati and Hamilton County, Cincinnati
OU   Ohio State University, Columbus

PENNSYLVANIA
PBL   Lehigh University, Bethlehem
PBm   Bryn Mawr College, Bryn Mawr
PHi   Historical Society of Pennsylvania, Philadelphia
PMA   Allegheny College, Meadville
PPAmP   American Philosophical Society, Philadelphia
PPF   Franklin Institute, Philadelphia
PPG   German Society of Pennsylvania, Philadelphia
PPL   Library Company of Philadelphia
PPRF   Rosenbach Foundation, Philadelphia
PPULC   Union Library Catalogue of Pennsylvania, Philadelphia
PR   Reading Public Library

PENNSYLVANIA (*cont.*)

PU University of Pennsylvania, Philadelphia

PWcHi Chester County Historical Society, West Chester

RHODE ISLAND

RPJCB John Carter Brown Library, Providence

TEXAS

TxU University of Texas, Austin

UTAH

UU University of Utah, Salt Lake City

VIRGINIA

ViU University of Virginia, Charlottesville

BIBLIOGRAPHICAL DESCRIPTIONS

1

BAY PSALM BOOK.

The whole booke of Psalmes faithfully translated into English metre. : Whereunto is prefixed a discourse declaring not only the lawfullnes, but also the necessity of the heavenly ordinance of singing scripture Psalmes in the churches of God. . . .

[Cambridge, Mass.] : Imprinted [by Stephen Daye], 1640.

Collation: 18 cm. (4to): *⁴ 2*⁴ A–V⁴ W–2L⁴. [296] p.

Notes: Place of publication and printer's name taken from Evans. Errata statement at end.

References: JCB Lib. Cat., pre-1675, II:280; Evans 4; Holmes, *Minor Mathers*, 53-A; Church, *Discovery*, 445; Sabin 66428; STC 2738.

JCB Library copy: Acq: 04606. Acquired in 1881. This copy is bound in contemporary calf and contains the signature of Richard Mather, one of its translators.

Copies: DLC, MWA, NN, CtY, RPJCB, MH, MB (2 copies), CSmH, PPRF, Bodleian Library.

5

BIBLE. German. Luther. 1743.

Biblia, : das ist : Die Heilige Schrift Altes und Neues Testaments, nach der deutschen Uebersetzung D. Martin Luthers, mit jedes Capitels kurtzen Summarien, auch beygefügten vielen und richtigen Parllelen [*sic*]; nebst einem Anhang des dritten und vierten Buchs Esrä und des dritten Buchs der Maccabäer.

Germantown : Gedruckt bey Christoph Saur, 1743.

Collation: 27 cm. (4to): v. [1]: π² A–6I⁴ 6K² (π1ᵛ, 6K2ᵛ blank); v. [2]: A–2L⁴ 2M⁶. 2v. bound in 1 (v. [1]: [4], 995, [1] p.; v. [2]: 277, [7] p.)

Notes: "The earliest Bible in a European language printed in America. Luther's version. A reprint of the Halle Bible (34th) edition, with the books 3 and 4 Esdras and 3 Maccabees supplied from the Berlenburg Bible . . ."—Darlow. Title page v. [2]: Das Neue Testament unsers Herrn und Heylandes Jesu Christi; verteutscht von Dr. Martin Luther. Mit jedes Capitels kurtzen Sumarien, auch bey gefügten vielen richtigen Parallelen. Germantown: Gedruckt und zu finden bey Christoph Saur, 1743. There are three variant states of the title page: variant 1 as transcribed above; variant 2 has "nebst dem gewöhnlichen Anhang" for "nebst einem Anhang" and "Parllelen" is corrected to "Parallelen"; variant 3 makes no mention of the "Anhang" at all, title ends "Parllelen."

References: Sabin 5191; Seidensticker, *German printing*, p. 20; Hildeburn, *The issues of the press in Pennsylvania*, 804; Wright, *Early Bibles of America*, p. 28–50, 163, plate [3]; Darlow, *Holy Scripture*, 4240; Rumball-Petre, *America's first Bibles*, p. 14–37; O'Callaghan, *Holy Scriptures*, p. 22–23; Evans 5127, 5128; Bötte & Tannhof 47.

JCB Library copy: Acq: 5401. Acquired in 1909. This copy is imperfect: lacks gatherings π and A as well as leaves 5B2–3 and 6K2 in v. [1], gatherings 2K–2M in v. [2]. The lacking title page of v. [1] does not allow a decision on which of the three variants is represented by this copy. Copy bound in contemporary calf over wooden boards, with brass corners and (damaged) clasps; it also has leather straps at the top and bottom of the spine for removing Bible from the shelf.

Copies: MiU-C, PPG, RPJCB, N, OC, PR, MiD, MoSCS, MB, NNAB, NN, NCaS, NcWsW, NIC, PPL, DLC, OU, NcD, CtY, PBL, CSmH, MNF, MWiW-C, MnU, MWA, PHi.

2

BIBLE. Massachuset. Eliot. 1663.

Mamusse wunneetupanatamwe up-Biblum God naneeswe Nukkone Testament kah wonk Wusku Testament. / Ne quoshkinnumuk nashpe Wuttinneumoh Christ noh asoowesit John Eliot.

Cambridge [Mass.] : Printeuoop nashpe Samuel Green kah Marmaduke Johnson., 1663.

Collation: 19 cm. (4to): π² A–5L⁴ 5M² ²A–²N⁴ (²N4 blank). [936] p.

Notes: First edition of the first Bible printed in the New World, and the first example in history of the translation and printing of the entire Bible in a new language (Massachuset) as a means of evangelism. For a complete account of the variations in different copies of this work, see Pilling. Contains only the Old Testament, the metrical version of the Psalms, and the rules for Christian living (on last leaf).

References: JCB Lib. Cat., pre-1675, III:87; Sabin

(29)

22154; Wing B2755; Evans 73; Pilling, *Bib. Algonquian languages*, p. 150, no. 37.

JCB Library copy: Acq: 01891. Acquired in 1854. This copy lacks blank leaf (²N4) at end. The Library also has two copies of the separate issue of the New Testament containing the English title and dedication (Evans 64).

Copies: RPJCB, MiU-C, PPL, PPRF, NN, InU, MB, MH, MWelC, MWiW-C, MdBJ-G, NNC.

6

CICERO, MARCUS TULLIUS.

[Cato maior de senectute. English]

M. T. Cicero's Cato major, or his Discourse of old-age : with explanatory notes.

Philadelphia : Printed and sold by B. Franklin, MDCCXLIV. [1744]

Collation: 21 cm. (4to):)(⁴ A–V⁴ ( )(1ᵛ, V4ᵛ blank). viii, 159, [1] p.

Notes: Translation, by James Logan, of: Cato maior de senectute. Also edited by James Logan. First American edition, issue in quarto, first state (with typographical error "ony" for "only" on p. 27, line 5). Errata statement on p. vi. Includes index (to footnotes by James Logan). Preface by Benjamin Franklin (p. iii–vi).

References: Evans 5361; Hildeburn, *The issues of the press in Pennsylvania*, 868; Miller, *Benjamin Franklin's Philadelphia printing*, 347; JCB Lib., *Annual reports*, VI:1956, p. 10–14.

JCB Library copy: Acq: 31854. Acquired in 1956. This copy is bound in contemporary calf.

Copies: RPJCB, PPAmP, CtHT-W, MnU, MiU-C, CtY, MWA, MH, NN, N, NjP, PU, PBm, MHi, PPL, MB, ICN, DLC, PPULC, NHi, PPF, MWiW-C, PHi, TxU.

11

COLLEGE OF WILLIAM AND MARY.

The charter, and statutes, of the College of William and Mary, in Virginia. / In Latin and English.

Williamsburg : Printed by William Parks, M, DCC, XXXVI. [1736]

Collation: 20 cm. (8vo): A–H⁸ (–H8) (E1ᵛ, E2ʳ, H6ᵛ, H7 blank). 121, [5] p.

Notes: Latin text on first, third, fifth and seventh leaves of each gathering; English text on second, fourth, sixth and eighth leaves of each gathering. Latin text translated from the English. English version of charter previously published as a section in Hartwell, Henry. The present state of Virginia, and the College, London, 1727, p. 72–95; cf. Evans, F. B. *The story of the Royal charter of the College of William and Mary.* Williamsburg, 1978 (Botetourt Publications, no. 4). Title vignette. Errata statement on p. [1–2] at end.

References: Sabin 104150; Clayton-Torrence, *A trial bib. of colonial Virginia*, 135; Berg, *18th cent. Williamsburg imprints*, 15; Bristol 992.

JCB Library copy: Acq: 5152. Acquired in 1909.

Copies: DLC, PHi, RPJCB, UU.

3

HUBBARD, WILLIAM, 1621 or 2–1704.

A narrative of the troubles with the Indians in New-England, from the first planting thereof in the year 1607. to this present year 1677. But chiefly of the late troubles in the last two years, 1675. and 1676. To which is added a discourse about the warre with the Pequods in the year 1637. / By W. Hubbard minister of Ipswich.

Boston; : Printed by John Foster, In the year 1677.

Collation: 19 cm. (4to): π² (π1+a⁴) χ1 B–L⁴ M⁶ m² O–R⁴ S² T⁴ n⁴ A–²L⁴ (π1ʳ blank). [14], 132, [8], 7–12, [2], 88 p., [1] folded leaf of plates : 1 map.

Notes: For a discussion of the numerous states of this edition, see: Adams, R. G. "William Hubbard's 'Narrative,' 1677." (In: *Papers of the Bibliographical Society of America* 33 (1939): 25–39). The map of New England, probably cut by John Foster, was the first map produced in the British colonies. For a discussion of the "White Hills" and "Wine Hills" variants, see Adams's article cited above. Errors in paging. Errata statements on p. [14], 1st count, and p. 88 at end. Issued with: The happiness of a people / William Hubbard, Boston, 1676, with special title page and separate paging and signatures.

References: J. C. Brown, Cat., 1493–1800, II:852; J. C. Brown, Cat., 1482–1700, II:1168; JCB Lib., *Annual reports*, II:1930, p. 29; Sabin 33445; Evans 231; Church, *Discovery*, 650; Wing H3210; Green, *John Foster*, p. 73–79.

JCB Library copies: Acq (variant 1): 15484. Acquired in 1929. Acq (variant 2): 01906. Acquired in 1854. Variant 1 contains the "White Hills" map and is bound in contemporary calf; variant 2 lacks the map and leaf π1 (license).

Copies: MH, CtY, MWA, ICN, ViU, InU, NHi, RPJCB, PPL, CtHT-W, DLC, MWiW-C, MiU-C, NIC, MB, PHi, NNC, NjP.

12

JEFFERSON, THOMAS, 1743–1826.

A summary view of the rights of British America. : Set forth in some resolutions intended for the inspection of the present delegates of the people of Virginia. Now in convention. / By a native, and member of the House of Burgesses.

Williamsburg : Printed by Clementina Rind, [1774].

Collation: 20 cm. (8vo): [A]⁴ B–C⁴ ([A]2ᵛ, C4ᵛ blank). 23, [1] p.

Notes: Author's name taken from Sabin and Boyd; cf. Boyd, J. P. "Historical and bibliographical notes on 'A summary view.' " (In: *The papers of Thomas Jefferson*, 1:669–676). Very likely published late in August 1774.

References: Evans 13350; Adams, *Amer. pamphlets*, 119a; Adams, *Brit. pamphlets*, 74–37a; Sabin 35918; Berg, *18th cent. Williamsburg imprints*, 218; Clayton-Torrence, *A trial bib. of colonial Virginia*, 418.

JCB Library copy: Acq: 15130. Acquired in 1928.

Copies: DLC, ViU, PPL, PHi, RPJCB, CSmH.

7

A Manual of Catholic prayers.

Philadelphia. : Printed for the subscribers, by Robert Bell, bookseller, in Third Street., MDCCLXXIV. [1774]

Collation: 16 cm. (12mo): [A]⁶ [B⁴ (–B4)]? C–2A⁶. 282 p. : ill.

Notes: Probably published by Rev. Robert Molyneux, pastor of St. Joseph's, Philadelphia; cf. Parsons. Preceded by: Proposals for printing by subscription, The Catholic Christian instructed. In the sacraments, sacrifice, ceremonies, and observances of the Church. By way of question and answer. / By R[ichard] C[halloner], Philadelphia, 1774, p. [1–4].

References: Evans 13588; Finotti, *Bib. catholica americana*, p. 16; Parsons, *Catholic Americana*, 25.

JCB Library copy: Acq: 30892. Acquired in 1951. This copy is bound in contemporary sheep, and lacks gathering [B]?, p. [13–18]?

Copies: RPJCB, DGU, PWᶜHi, ICN.

10

MARKLAND, JOHN.

Typographia. : An ode, on printing.

Williamsburg : Printed by William Parks., M,DCC, XXX. [1730]

Collation: 23 cm. (4to): [A]² B–D² ([A]1ᵛ, D2ᵛ blank). iv, 5–15, [1] p.

Notes: Author's name given at end of dedication (p. iv) as: J. Markland. The first book printed in the American colonies which relates to the art of printing.

References: Evans 3298; Clayton-Torrence, *A trial bib. of colonial Virginia*, 114; Berg, *18th cent. Williamsburg imprints*, 2.

JCB Library copy: Acq: 04439. Acquired in 1899.

Copies: RPJCB.

8

NEW YORK (N.Y.)

The charter of the city of New-York; / printed by order of the mayor, recorder, aldermen and commonalty of the city aforesaid. To which is annexed, the act of the General Assembly confirming the same.

New-York, : Printed by John Peter Zenger., 1735.

Collation: 32 cm. (fol.): π1 A–M² χ1 (π1ᵛ blank). 52 p.

Notes: Charter granted by Governor John Montgomerie which is dated 15 Jan. 1730. A previous charter granted by Governor Thomas Dongan on 22 April 1686 was published in New York, 1720. Pages 12–13 misnumbered 10–11. "An act for confirming into the city of New-York its rights and privileges" (p. 51–52).

References: Evans 3942; Sabin 54165; Rutherfurd, *John Peter Zenger*, p. 152–153; JCB Lib., *Annual reports*, II:1926, p. 5, 11.

JCB Library copy: Acq: 14497–1. Acquired in 1926. This copy is bound in contemporary paper wrappers.

Copies: RPJCB, NN, NHi, DLC, InU, NjP, CSmH, PPL, N.

4

PENNSYLVANIA (Colony).

[Laws, etc.]

The laws of the Province of Pensilvania collected into one volumn [*sic*], / by order of the Governour and Assembly of the said province.

[Philadelphia] : Printed & sold by Andr. Bradford in Philadelphia, 1714.

Collation: 33 cm. (fol.): π² [A]² B–U² W² X–2T² 2U² (–2U2). [4], 32, 34–37, 43 [i.e. 39]–58, 69–94 [i.e. 100], 99–184 p.

Notes: First printed collection of the laws of Pennsylvania, beginning with 1700. Numerous errors in paging; altogether 178 pages present.

References: Evans 1712; Sabin 60192; Hildeburn, *The issues of the press in Pennsylvania*, 128.

JCB Library copy: Acq: 467. Acquired in 1904. This copy is bound in contemporary calf, and contains numerous ms. annotations.

Copies: NNC, CSmH, PPL, NN, MH, MB, MH-L, RPJCB.

9

SABBATH PRAYERS (Sephardic). English.
Prayers for Shabbath, Rosh-Hashanah, and Kippur, : or, The Sabbath, the begining [*sic*] of the year, and the Day of Atonements; with the Amidah and Musaph of the Moadim, or solemn seasons. According to the order of the Spanish and Portuguese Jews. / Translated by Isaac Pinto.

[New York] : And for him printed by John Holt, in New-York., A.M. 5526. [i.e. 1765–1766]

Collation: 19 cm. (4to): [A]² B–2B⁴ (2B4ᵛ blank). iv, 190, [2] p.

Notes: Errata statement on p. [1], at end.

References: Evans 10343; Sabin 62992; Murphy, *John Holt*, 45.

JCB Library copy: Acq: 30682. Acquired in 1950. This copy is bound in contemporary calf, rebacked.

Copies: MB, PMA, RPJCB.

CHECKLIST

of the Seventy-three Items in the Original "Book in the Americas" Exhibition

[36] ACOSTA, JOSÉ DE (1540–1600). *De natura Novi Orbis*. Cologne, 1596.

[18] ALEMÁN, MATEO (1547–1614?). *Ortografia castellana*. Mexico, 1609.

[19] ALEMÁN, MATEO (1547–1614?). *Sucesos de D. frai Garcia Gera arcobispo de Mejico*. Mexico, 1613.

[6] ALPHONSUS, A VERA CRUCE (ca. 1504–1584). *Dialectica resolutio*. Mexico, 1554.

[6] ALPHONSUS, A VERA CRUCE (ca. 1504–1584). *Phisica, speculatio*. Mexico, 1557.

[6] ALPHONSUS, A VERA CRUCE (ca. 1504–1584). *Recognitio, summularum*. Mexico, 1554.

[65] ARAUJO, ANTONIO DE (1566–1632). *Catecismo brasilico de doutrina christãa*. Lisbon, 1686.

[20] BECERRA TANCO, LUIS (1602–1672). *Felicidad de Mexico*. Mexico, 1675.

[2] BIEL, GABRIEL (d. 1495). *Repertorium generale & succinctum*. Lyons, 1527.

[71] BRAZIL. *Decreto. Tendo-me constado, que os prélos, que se achão nesta capital*. [Rio de Janeiro, 1811].

[67] CAMÕES, LUÍS DE (1524?–1580). *Os Lusiadas*. Lisbon, 1572.

[44] CARRIÓ DE LA VANDERA, ALONSO (b. ca. 1706). *El lazarillo de ciegos caminantes desde Buenos-Ayres, hasta Lima*. Gijón [Lima], [1775 or 1776].

[7] CASAS, BARTOLOMÉ DE LAS (1474–1566). *Breuissima relacion de la destruycion de las Indias*. Seville, [1553].

[8] CASAS, BARTOLOMÉ DE LAS (1474–1566). *Narratio regionum indicarum per Hispanos quosdam deuastatarum verissima*. Frankfurt, 1598.

[27] CATHOLIC CHURCH. *Missa Gothica seù Mozarabica*. Puebla de los Angeles [Mexico], 1770.

[34] CATHOLIC CHURCH. *Tercero cathecismo y exposicion de la doctrina christiana*. Ciudad de los Reyes [Lima], 1585.

[10] CATHOLIC CHURCH. [*Testerian catechism*]. [Mexico, 18th century].

[32] CIEZA DE LEÓN, PEDRO DE (1518–1560). *Parte primera dela chronica del Peru*. Seville, 1553.

[12] CIUDAD REAL, ANTONIO DE (1551–1617). [*Maya-Spanish and Spanish-Maya dictionary: the Diccionario de Motul*]. [Mexico, after 1577: probably ca. 1600–1630].

[60] COMPAÑÍA DE MARÍA SANTÍSIMA DE LA ENSEÑANZA DE MÉXICO. *Relacion historica de la fundacion de este Convento de Nuestra Señora del Pilar*. Mexico, 1793.

[26] CORTÉS, HERNÁN (1485–1547). *Historia de Nueva-España*. Mexico, 1770.

[25] [*Coyoacán Codex. Pictorial codex in the Nahuatl language*]. [Mexico, ca. 1700 to before 1743].

[66] CUNHA, LUIS ANTÓNIO ROSADO DA. *Relaçaõ da entrada que fez o excellentissimo, e reverendissimo senhor D. Fr. Antonio do Desterro Malheyro*. Rio de Janeiro, [1747].

[39] ERCILLA Y ZÚÑIGA, ALONSO DE (1533–1594). *La Araucana*. Madrid, 1590.

[57] FIDALGO DELVAS. *Relaçam verdadeira dos trabalhos q[ue] ho gouernador do[m] Ferna[n]do d[e] Souto [e] certos fidalgos portugueses passarom*. Evora, 1557.

[70] GAMA, JOSÉ BASILIO DA (1740–1795). *O Uraguay*. Lisbon, 1769.

[53] GARRIGA, ANTONIO (1662–1733). *Instruccion practica para ordenar santamente la vidà*. Loreto, 1713.

[4] GERSON, JEAN (1363–1429). *Tripartito del christianissimo y consolatorio doctor Juan Gerson de doctrina christiana*. Mexico, 1544.

[11] GILBERTI, MATURINO (1498–1585). *Dialogo de doctrina christiana, enla lengua d[e] Mechuaca[n]*. Mexico, 1559.

[69] GONZAGA, TOMÁS ANTÔNIO (1744–1807?). *Marilia de Dirceo*. Lisbon, 1819–[1820].

[72] GUIMARÃES, MANUEL FERREIRA DE ARAUJO (1777–1838). *Elementos de astronomia*. Rio de Janeiro, [1814].

[17] HERNÁNDEZ, FRANCISCO (1514–1587). *Quatro libros. De la naturaleza, y virtudes de las plantas, y animales que estan receuidos en el vso de medicina en la Nueua España*. Mexico, 1615.

[64] JESUITS. *Auisi particolari delle Indie di Portugallo*. Rome, 1552.

[24] JUANA INÉS DE LA CRUZ (1648–1695). *Carta athenagorica*. Puebla de los Angeles [Mexico], 1690.

[23] JUANA INÉS DE LA CRUZ (1648–1695). *Villancicos*. Mexico, [1677].

[21] KINO, EUSEBIO FRANCISCO (1644–1711). *Exposicion astronomica de el cometa*. Mexico, 1681.

[29] LOBO, MANUEL (1612–1686). *Relacion de la vida, y virtudes del V. hermano Pedro de San Ioseph Betancur*. Guatemala, 1667.

[73] LUCCOCK, JOHN. *Notes on Rio de Janeiro, and the southern parts of Brazil*. London, 1820.

[61] MASÚSTEGUI, PEDRO. *Arte de construccion*. Santa Fé [de Bogotá], 1784.

[3] MEDINA, MIGUEL DE (1489–1578). *De sacrorum hominum continentia libri V*. Venice, 1569.

[45] *Mercurio peruano de historia, literatura, y noticias públicas*. Lima, [1791]–1795.

[28] MEXICO. *Decreto constitucional para la libertad de la America mexicana*. [Apatzingán, 1814].

[15] MONARDES, NICOLÁS (ca. 1512–1588). *Dos libros. : El vno trata de todas las cosas q[ue] trae[n] de n[uest]ras Indias Occide[n]tales, que siruen al vso de medicina*. Seville, 1565.

[16] MONARDES, NICOLÁS (ca. 1512–1588). *Ioyfull nevves out of the newe founde worlde*. London, 1577.

[46] *El Monitor Araucano*. Santiago, 1813–1814.

[5] NEW SPAIN. *Ordena[n]ças y copilacion de leyes: hechas por el muy illustre señor don Antonio d[e] Me[n]doça*. Mexico, 1548.

[31] *Noticia del establecimiento del museo de esta capital de la Nueva Guatemala*. [Guatemala], 1797.

[56] NÚÑEZ CABEZA DE VACA, ALVAR (16th cent). *La relacion . . . de lo acaescido en las Indias*. [Zamora, 1542].

[40] OÑA, PEDRO DE (1570?–1643?). *Arauco domado*. Ciudad de los Reyes [Lima], 1596.

[41] OÑA, PEDRO DE (1570?–1643?). *Temblor de Lima año de 1609*. Lima, 1609.

[62] PARRA, ANTONIO. *Descripcion de diferentes piezas de historia natural*. Havana, 1787.

[37] PERU. *Ordencas [sic] qve el señor marqves de Cañete visorey de estos reynos del Piru mando hazer para el remedio de los excessos*. Ciudad de los Reyes [Lima], [1594].

[68] PIMENTA, MIGUEL DÍAS (ca. 1661–1715). *Noticias do que he o achaque do bicho*. Lisbon, 1707.

[52] RUIZ DE MONTOYA, ANTONIO (1585–1652). *Arte de la lengua guarani*. Santa María la Mayor, 1724.

[50] RUIZ DE MONTOYA, ANTONIO (1585–1652). *Arte, y bocabulario de la lengua guarani*. Madrid, 1640.

[49] RUIZ DE MONTOYA, ANTONIO (1585–1652). *Catecismo de la lengua guarani*. Madrid, 1640.

[48] RUIZ DE MONTOYA, ANTONIO (1585–1652). *Señor*. [Madrid, 1639 or 1640].

[51] RUIZ DE MONTOYA, ANTONIO (1585–1652). *Vocabulario de la lengua guarani*. Santa María la Mayor, 1722.

[30] SÁENZ OVECURI, DIEGO. *Thomasiada al sol de la iglesia, y su doctor santo Thomas de Aquino*. Guatemala, 1667.

[13]   Sahagún, Bernardino de (d. 1590). *Psalmodia christiana*. Mexico, 1583.

[55]   San Alberto, José Antonio de (1727–1804). *Carta circular, ò edicto*. Buenos Aires, 1781.

[47]   San Martín, José de (1778–1850). *Proclama a los habitantes del estado de Chile*. [Santiago, 1820].

[59]   Sigüenza y Góngora, Carlos de (1645–1700). *Descripcion, que de la vaia de Santa Maria de Galve (antes Pansacola)*. [Madrid? ca. 1720].

[22]   Sigüenza y Góngora, Carlos de (1645–1700). *Libra astronomica*. Mexico, 1690.

[9]   Spain. *Leyes y ordenanças nueuame[n]te hechas por Su Magestad, p[ar]a la gouernacion de las Indias y buen tratamiento y conseruacion de los indios*. Alcalá de Henares, 1543.

[33]   Spain. *Pragmatica sobre los diez dias del año*. Ciudad de los Reyes [Lima], 1584.

[43]   Suárez de Figueroa, Miguel. *Templo de N. grande patriarca San Francisco de la provincia de los doze apostoles de el Peru*. Lima, 1675.

[14]   Tovar, Juan de (ca. 1546–ca. 1626). *Historia de la benida de los yndios*. [Mexico, between 1582 and 1587].

[38]   Universidad Nacional Mayor de San Marcos. *Constituciones y ordenancas de la Vniuersidad*. Ciudad de los Reyes [Lima], 1602.

[35]   Valdivia, Luis de (1561–1642). *Doctrina christiana y cathecismo en la lengua allentiac*. Lima, 1607.

[58]   Vega, Garcilaso de la (1539–1616). *La Florida del Ynca. Historia del adelantado Hernando de Soto*. Lisbon, 1605.

[42]   Vega, Garcilaso de la (1539–1616). *Primera parte de los commentarios reales*. Lisbon, 1609.

[63]   Venezuela. *Constitucion federal, para los estados de Venezuela*. Caracas, 1812.

[54]   Yapuguay, Nicolas. *Sermones y exemplos en lengua guarani*. Pueblo de San Francisco Xavier, 1727.

[1]   Zumárraga, Juan de (1468–1548). *Dotrina breue muy p[ro]uechosa delas cosas q[ue] p[er]tenecen ala fe catholica y a n[uest]ra cristiandad*. Mexico, [1544].

DESIGNED, COMPOSED, PRINTED & BOUND

BY MERIDEN-STINEHOUR PRESS

LUNENBURG, VERMONT